GIANTS OF THE OLD TESTAMENT

LESSONS ON LIVING FROM

MOSES

The Practice of God's Presence

A devotional by
WOODROW KROLL

BACK TO THE BIBLE®
Lincoln, Nebraska

MOSES—THE PRACTICE
OF GOD'S PRESENCE
published by Back to the Bible
©1997 by Woodrow Kroll

International Standard Book Number
0-8474-0678-4

Edited by Rachel Derowitsch
Cover concept by Robert Greuter
& Associates

For information:
BACK TO THE BIBLE
POST OFFICE BOX 82808
LINCOLN, NEBRASKA 68501

1 2 3 4 5 6 7 8—03 02 01 00 99 98 97

Printed in the USA

CONTENTS

DAY 1

Exodus 24:1-2

*Now He said to Moses, "Come up to the
L*ORD*, you and Aaron, Nadab and Abihu, and
seventy of the elders of Israel, and worship
from afar. And Moses alone shall come near
the L*ORD*, but they shall not come near; nor
shall the people go up with him."*

Let Us Draw Near

In a cathedral in Copenhagen, Den-
mark, there is a magnificent statue of
Jesus by the noted sculptor Bertel Thorvaldsen. When first completed, the sculpture depicted Christ with His face looking
up and arms extended over His head. It
was a statue of the majestic, conquering
Christ. Later that night, however, before
the clay had hardened, sea mist seeped
into the studio. The sculpture was trans-
formed into a Christ with head bent forward and arms stretched downward, as if
in a pose of gentle invitation. At first Thorvaldsen was bitterly disappointed. But as
he studied the altered sculpture, he came
to see a dimension of Christ that had not
been real to him before —the Christ who is
a gentle, merciful Savior. On the base of
the completed statue Thorvaldsen
inscribed the words, "Come Unto Me."

When Israel came to Mount Sinai, God
called the leaders of the people to "come
unto me," but they were still to "worship

4

from afar." Only Moses was allowed to come close and have fellowship with the Lord.

In the New Testament, however, all believers are invited to have an intimate relationship with God. In fact, the writer of Hebrews urges us, "And having a High Priest over the house of God, let us *draw near* with a true heart in full assurance of faith" (Heb. 10:21-22, italics mine). James records the promise, "Draw near to God and He will draw near to you" (James 4:8).

Don't keep your distance from God. He wants you to draw close. The Father says, "Come!" (Isa. 1:18). Jesus says, "Come!" (Matt. 11:28). The Spirit says, "Come!" (Rev. 22:17). Confess your sins first and be right with Him. Then enjoy the blessings of an intimate relationship with your Heavenly Father.

God's heart is as open to you as His arms.

Reflections/Prayer Requests

_____

_____

_____

_____

_____

_____

DAY 2

Exodus 24:3, 7

So Moses came and told the people all the words of the LORD and all the judgments. And all the people answered with one voice and said, "All the words which the LORD has said we will do."
Then he took the Book of the Covenant and read in the hearing of the people. And they said, "All that the LORD has said we will do, and be obedient."

Trust and Obey

A television news crew was on assignment in southern Florida in August 1992 filming the widespread destruction of Hurricane Andrew. One scene showed a neighborhood with only one house remaining on its foundation. A reporter approached the owner and asked, "Why is your house the only one still standing?" The man responded, "I built the house myself, and I built it according to the Florida state building code. When the code called for 2' x 6' roof trusses, I used 2' x 6' trusses. I was told that a house built according to code could withstand a hurricane and mine did. I suppose no one else followed the code."

When Moses shared God's "code" of conduct with the people, their first response was an unqualified, "All the words which the LORD has said we will do." Unfortunately, like many of us today, they failed to follow through on their commitment and the consequences were ultimately devastating.

God's standards are not given to spoil our fun but to protect us from the storms of life. The key to surviving life's trials and experiencing maximum joy is to trust God and obey His Word. Remember the words of the old hymn: "Trust and obey, for there's no other way to be happy in Jesus, but to trust and obey."

If Satan is tempting you to disobey God and His Word, remind yourself that every life has its storms. The only way to survive them safely and joyfully is to make sure your life is built according to the code.

A life built by the code will never crumble during the storms.

Reflections/Prayer Requests

_____

_____

_____

_____

_____

_____

_____

_____

DAY 3

Exodus 24:12, 18

*Then the L*ORD *said to Moses, "Come up to
Me on the mountain and be there; and I will
give you tablets of stone, and the law and
commandments which I have written,
that you may teach them."
So Moses went into the midst of the cloud
and went up into the mountain.
And Moses was on the mountain
forty days and forty nights.*

Time With God

The busyness of life affects just about
everything, even the classics. One theater
is offering an abridged version of Shake-
speare's works. If you don't have time to
view each of them separately, you can see
37 of the Bard's plays condensed into one
act and experience a rewrite of *Hamlet* in
the second.

Moses also was a busy man. He was
responsible for the lives and welfare of
more than a million people. He was the
primary liaison between God and those
under his care. Even though Aaron and
his sons had been appointed priests (Ex.
28:41), Moses was the one who spoke to
God face to face (33:7-11). At one point,
Jethro, Moses' father-in-law, became so
concerned about him that he recommend-
ed Moses delegate some of his responsibilities to others. Yet Moses wasn't con-

tent to settle for an abridged relationship with God. He took 40 days and 40 nights from his busy schedule to spend with the Lord.

Christians today often use busyness to explain why they don't have time for such spiritual disciplines as prayer or Bible study. As they rush to get to the end of their lives, they fill their hours with work, sports, family and social activities. If they're lucky, they manage to squeeze a bit of God into the cracks between everything else.

But life would be more meaningful if we learned to reverse the process. Fill your life with God, and you'll still have time for everything else that's important. It might amaze you how much you could accomplish if you put God first. The busier you become, the more important it is that you spend quality time with God.

If Satan can't make you bad, he'll make you busy.

Reflections/Prayer Requests

_____

_____

_____

_____

_____

DAY 4

Exodus 25:1-2

Then the LORD spoke to Moses, saying: "Speak to the children of Israel, that they bring Me an offering. From everyone who gives it willingly with his heart you shall take My offering."

A Willing Gift

A careless Scot once tossed a crown into the collection plate thinking it was a penny. When he saw his mistake, he asked to have it back. The deacon refused, and then the Scot grunted, "Aweel, aweel, I'll get credit for it in heaven." The deacon responded, "Na, na, ye'll get credit for the penny."

God makes it clear that the only gifts He desires are those given with a willing heart. When He gave the instructions for building His tabernacle, He specifically stated that Moses was to accept building materials only from the one "who gives it willingly with his heart."

This same truth is repeated in 2 Corinthians 9:7: "So let each one give as he purposes in his heart, not grudgingly or of necessity; for God loves a cheerful giver." The Greek word translated "cheerful" is the root for the English word "hilarious." Giving to God is not just a "good" feeling; it's an overflowing, boisterous, lively experience.

Our offering made to God is a responsibility (1 Cor. 16:2), but it's much more. It's a joy that comes close to ecstasy. To return even a small amount to God, who gave everything to us, is cause for rejoicing.

Look for an opportunity today to give to God. Whether you give your time, your talent or your material resources, everything given with an attitude of joyful willingness is always acceptable to God.

The attitude of the giver is an essential part of the gift.

Reflections/Prayer Requests

DAY 5

Exodus 25:22

And there I will meet with you, and I will speak with you from above the mercy seat, from between the two cherubim which are on the ark of the Testimony, of all things which I will give you in commandment to the children of Israel.

At the Mercy Seat

A famous artist was commissioned to paint the portrait of a wealthy lady. After weeks of labor, the painting was ready for viewing. The painter removed the covering from the picture for her inspection. Observing his work, the lady said disdainfully, "I don't believe you have done me justice." "Madam," the artist replied, "I don't believe you want justice; you want mercy."

God gave Moses very detailed instructions not only on the building of the tabernacle, but also for every piece of furniture that was to go in it. Included in the furnishings was the Ark of the Covenant. It was just a box approximately 45 inches long, 27 inches wide and 27 inches high, but it was covered with gold (v. 10). This ark was placed in the Holy of Holies, an area of the tabernacle where God manifested Himself in a special way. On top of it was a lid of pure gold with a golden cherub at each end. This lid was called the mercy seat.

When Moses met with God at the Ark of the Covenant, his thoughts were not on justice; they were on mercy. In later years, as pilgrims made their way to the temple, they sang, "If You, LORD, should mark iniquities . . . who could stand?" (Ps. 130:3). When we come before God, our goal is not to find justice—our heart's cry is for mercy.

Today as you meet with God, ask for His unlimited mercy. The Bible says, "Let us therefore come boldly to the throne of grace, that we may obtain mercy and find grace to help in time of need" (Heb. 4:16). Look to God's mercy and you'll never be disappointed.

Jesus endured the pain of God's justice so we could enjoy the pleasure of God's mercy.

Reflections/Prayer Requests

DAY 6

Exodus 32:1

Now when the people saw that Moses delayed coming down from the mountain, the people gathered together to Aaron, and said to him, "Come, make us gods that shall go before us; for as for this Moses, the man who brought us up out of the land of Egypt, we do not know what has become of him."

Weary of Waiting

Archibald Rutledge wrote that one day he met a man whose dog had just been killed in a forest fire. Heartbroken, the man explained to Rutledge how it happened. Because he worked outdoors, he often took his dog with him. That morning he left the animal in a clearing and gave him a command to stay and watch his lunch pail. A fire started in the woods, and soon the blaze spread to the spot where the dog had been left. But he didn't move. He waited right where he was and perished.

The Israelites, on the other hand, quickly grew weary of waiting. Moses had been gone only 40 days when they began to pressure Aaron to find "gods" that could lead them into the Promised Land. Their only thought was of the pleasures that awaited them in a land "flowing with milk and honey." They grew restless under the need to wait.

Christians face the same temptation. Often we are eager to get on with it. We have so much to do; so many tasks beckon us forward. We don't want to sit and wait, so we lurch forward with gods of our own making. We use our own wisdom and strength to try to reach goals that only God is adequate to achieve.

If you find yourself straining to go forward when God doesn't seem to be in a hurry, hold back and wait. Perhaps He has an entirely different plan for your life. Concentrate on what you must do now and let God move you ahead when the time is right.

Wait on God and want for nothing.

Reflections/Prayer Requests

_____

_____

_____

_____

_____

_____

_____

_____

_____

_____

DAY 7

Exodus 32:11, 14

*Then Moses pleaded with the LORD his God,
and said: "LORD, why does Your wrath burn
hot against Your people whom You have
brought out of the land of Egypt with great
power and with a mighty hand?"
So the LORD relented from the harm which He
said He would do to His people.*

Lift Up Holy Hands

A young boy was browsing through his
father's books. He found a story that
seemed interesting and decided he would
read it. At the same time, many miles
away, his mother felt especially burdened
for her son. She found a solitary spot and
began to intercede with God for his salvation. Hour after hour passed while that
mother stayed upon her knees, until her
heart was assured that her prayers were
heard. When she returned home, the
mother found that the boy had been saved
that afternoon. That boy was Hudson Tay-
lor, who became one of the world's most
renown missionaries.

Moses' intercessory prayer earned him
an equally rich reward: the lives of his
people. Their wickedness and disobedience had reached such a degree that God
was ready to replace them with others of
Moses' line. Moses so earnestly prayed,

however, that God relented and the people were spared.

Intercessory prayer—praying for others—is one of the greatest privileges Christians can exercise. Paul urges that "supplications, prayers, intercessions, and giving of thanks be made for all men, for kings and all who are in authority" (1 Tim. 2:1-2). James exhorts us to "pray for one another" (James 5:16).

British Bible teacher J. Sidlow Baxter observed, "Men may spurn our appeal, reject our message, oppose our arguments, despise our persons, but they are helpless against our prayers."

In your prayer time, set aside a few moments to pray for those who have special responsibilities or special needs. Ask God to make you an earnest intercessor for His glory.

Jesus is interceding for you. Can you do less for others?

Reflections/Prayer Requests

_____

_____

_____

_____

_____

DAY 8

Exodus 32:25-26

Now when Moses saw that the people were unrestrained (for Aaron had not restrained them, to their shame among their enemies), then Moses stood in the entrance of the camp, and said, "Whoever is on the LORD's side, let him come to me." And all the sons of Levi gathered themselves together to him.

No Fence-sitting Allowed

Fence-sitting can be hazardous, like it was for the New York family who bought a ranch out West, where they intended to raise cattle. One day a friend from back East visited and asked if the ranch had a name. "Well," said the would-be cattle-man, "I wanted to name it the Bar-J. My wife favored Suzy-Q, one son liked the Flying-W, and the other wanted the Lazy-Y. So we're calling it the Bar-J-Suzy-Q-Fly-ing-W-Lazy-Y." "But where are all your cattle?" the friend asked. "Unfortunately," the man replied, "none of them survived the branding."

Moses allowed no such fence-sitting. When he came down from Mount Sinai and found the camp in an uproar, he threw down a challenge. A choice had to be made. Either the people were on the Lord's side or they weren't. There was no middle ground.

Too many Christians like to sit on the fence. They want one foot in the faith and the other foot in the world. They don't want to stand out too sharply from unbelievers for fear of negative responses. They like to fit in. But, on the other hand, they don't want to be excluded from believers' fellowship either. They really don't know what to do, so they take a prominent position on the fence.

If you've been sitting on the fence, isn't it time you *stood* for something? Consider Moses' challenge to his people. Make a choice. Either take your stand for the Lord or side with the world. Whatever you do, don't straddle the fence. You won't find any of God's heroes there.

If you sit on the fence, expect to get splinters.

Reflections/Prayer Requests

_____

_____

_____

_____

_____

_____

_____

_____

DAY 9

Exodus 32:27-28

*And he said to them, "Thus says the L*ord *God of Israel: 'Let every man put his sword on his side, and go in and out from entrance to entrance throughout the camp, and let every man kill his brother, every man his companion, and every man his neighbor.'" So the sons of Levi did according to the word of Moses. And about three thousand men of the people fell that day.*

Trifling With God

D. L. Moody once warned, "Go play with forked lightening, go trifle with pestilence and disease, but trifle not with God." A relationship with the living God is a wonderful thing, but it must never be taken lightly.

The Israelites discovered that, much to their sorrow. God had communicated His standards to them (Ex. 20) and the people responded, "All that the Lord has said we will do, and be obedient" (24:7). Yet only a short time later, while Moses was with God on Mount Sinai, they convinced Aaron to make an idol of gold. Then the people of God engaged in sexual debauchery (32:6). Such disregard toward God's principles was met with swift and horrible consequences. About three thousand men were put to death by the avenging swords of the Levites.

The church today is often guilty of equal flippancy. Someone has observed, "Most middle-class Americans tend to worship their work, to work at their play and to play at their worship." Can such an attitude avoid God's judgment?

Ask God to help you deepen your commitment to His standards. Pray as David did, "Search me, O God, and know my heart . . . and see if there is any wicked way in me" (Ps. 139:23-24). Commit yourself to love the Lord your God with all your heart and soul and mind. It's the direct path to purity and the power of God.

When you play games with God, you always lose.

Reflections/Prayer Requests

_____

_____

_____

_____

_____

_____

_____

_____

_____

_____

DAY 10

Exodus 33:14-15

And He said, "My Presence will go with you, and I will give you rest." Then he said to Him, "If Your Presence does not go with us, do not bring us up from here."

The Importance of His Presence

Throughout the Christian era, godly men and women have testified to the importance of God's presence in their lives. In 1859 John G. Paton arrived in the New Hebrides islands as a missionary. A short time later his wife died in childbirth. Paton had to bury the bodies of his wife and newborn child in unmarked graves in the middle of the night to keep them from cannibals. He wrote of that heart-wrenching experience, "I must need have gone mad by that lonely grave but for the presence of Jesus Christ."

In the late 1950s, 23-year-old Armando Valladares was thrown into a Cuban prison, where he remained for 22 years. Executions were staged each night during his first year in prison. Later, he endured some of the most vile and sadistic tortures imaginable. In his memoirs, *Against All Hope*, Valladares wrote, "I sought God.... I never asked Him to get me out of there.... I only prayed for Him to accompany me."

Moses prayed for the same thing. In fact, he said, "Lord, if You're not going to be with us, then let's just quit right here." Without God's presence, Moses saw no value in going on.

If you're discouraged, facing trials or dealing with sorrow, take comfort in the assurance that God is with you. You *can* go on because God will walk beside you every step of the way. Ask Him to make His presence known to you today; trust that He is always with you. That's His promise to you!

God's presence doesn't make life easy, just worthwhile.

Reflections/Prayer Requests

_____

_____

_____

_____

_____

_____

_____

_____

_____

_____

DAY 11

Exodus 33:21-23

And the LORD said, "Here is a place by Me, and you shall stand on the rock. So it shall be, while My glory passes by, that I will put you in the cleft of the rock, and will cover you with My hand while I pass by. Then I will take away My hand, and you shall see My back; but My face shall not be seen."

In the Cleft of the Rock

In the March 1776 issue of *The Gospel Magazine*, Augustus Toplady maintained that if a man lived to the age of 80, he would have the opportunity to commit more than two and a half billion sins. Obviously it would be impossible for a person to pay for all those sins. Therefore, Toplady offered this solution in a hymn he wrote. He pled, "Rock of Ages, cleft for me, let me hide myself in Thee."

Moses found that this was his solution also. Sinful as he was, he had a great longing to see God more fully, to know Him more intimately. But the sinfulness of man and the glory of God could not coexist. To see God in all His glory would have meant instantaneous annihilation for Moses. So God provided a compromise. He placed Moses in a fissure of a rock and protected him as His glory passed by. Then God allowed him to see the "afterglow" of His presence.

24

Deep in all of our hearts lies the longing to see God more fully, to discover His presence to a greater degree. But there is also an innate fear because we know, and rightly so, that we cannot exist in the presence of His unapproachable glory.

If you desire this in your heart, remember the rest of what Toplady wrote in the hymn that would become "Rock of Ages." He continued, "Let the water and the blood, from Thy riven side which flowed, be of sin the double cure; save me from its guilt and power." Confess your sins to God, ask Him to cleanse you with the blood of Christ, and enjoy a deeper sense of God's glory.

Only those hidden in God can safely see God revealed.

Reflections/Prayer Requests

_____

_____

_____

_____

_____

_____

_____

_____

_____

DAY 12

Exodus 36:1-2

And Bezaleel and Aholiab, and every gifted artisan in whom the LORD has put wisdom and understanding, to know how to do all manner of work for the service of the sanctuary, shall do according to all that the LORD has commanded. Then Moses called Bezaleel and Aholiab, and every gifted artisan in whose heart the LORD had put wisdom, everyone whose heart was stirred, to come and do the work.

Exercise Your Gift

A 38-year-old woman used to go to the movies and pine, "If only I had her looks." She would listen to a singer and moan, "If only I had her voice." Then one day a friend suggested she stop comparing herself with others and start concentrating on what she did have. The woman remembered that in high school she had a reputation for being the funniest girl around. She began to look for ways to use this ability. Before she retired, comedienne Phyllis Diller made more than a million dollars a year. She wasn't good-looking and she had a scratchy voice, but she used the gift she had.

When it was time to construct the tabernacle, God gave to each worker the ability needed to accomplish the task. There were those who worked with animal hides, those who cut and set jewels, those who worked with metal and many others whom He endowed with special wisdom and understanding. God called each to do his or her part in creating the tabernacle. By concentrating on the skill God gave them, they erected a magnificent structure that lasted for hundreds of years.

If you have received Christ as your Savior, the Holy Spirit also has given you a spiritual gift. It may not be one that puts you up front like teaching or preaching or singing in the choir, but your gift is essential nevertheless. Don't worry about the gifts you don't have; concentrate on the ones you do have. Ask God to help you use your spiritual gift in the most effective way possible for His glory.

What you have is God's gift to you; how you use it is your gift to God.

Reflections/Prayer Requests

_____

_____

_____

_____

_____

_____

_____

DAY 13

Leviticus 1:17

Then he shall split it at its wings, but shall not divide it completely; and the priest shall burn it on the altar, on the wood that is on the fire. It is a burnt sacrifice, an offering made by fire, a sweet aroma to the LORD.

A Sweet Aroma

Americans are in a battle against foul odors. We bathe with perfumed soaps, spray with aromatic aerosols and gargle with spicy liquids—all in an effort not to offend those we meet. All this is acceptable and appreciated, but what does it take to make an aroma that smells good to God?

As Moses met with God in the tabernacle, the Lord laid out detailed instructions for the various sacrifices His people should follow. He assured Moses that fulfilling these instructions would result in a "sweet aroma to the LORD." Obviously the odor of the burning sacrifice was not sweet. In fact, the smell of burning flesh and hair or feathers is rather offensive. The sweetness came from the attitudes of the one offering the sacrifice: humility (admitting he or she is a sinner in need of a sacrifice) and obedience (offering an acceptable sacrifice as directed by God).

These same attitudes are still important for us. While we no longer sacrifice animals, Paul urges us to "present [our] bodies a living sacrifice, holy, acceptable to God, which is [our] reasonable service" (Rom. 12:1). Paul calls for us to humbly and obediently surrender our lives to God as our sacrifice to Him—not just a part of ourselves, but our whole body.

While the Old Testament sacrifice had no say in the matter, you and I do. As the Lord speaks to you about His will for your life, will you voluntarily place yourself upon the altar of sacrifice? Humbly acknowledge His ownership of all that you are and have. Obediently respond to His Word and His will. If you make such an offering, it will not fail to be a sweet aroma to the Lord.

If you really want to please the Lord, let Him get a whiff of your obedience.

Reflections/Prayer Requests

_____

_____

_____

_____

_____

_____

DAY 14

Leviticus 10:1-2

*Then Nadab and Abihu, the sons of Aaron,
each took his censer and put fire in it,
put incense on it, and offered profane fire
before the L<small>ORD</small>, which He had not commanded them. So fire went out from the L<small>ORD</small>
and devoured them, and they died
before the L<small>ORD</small>.*

Doing Your Own Thing

A few years ago a research team study-
ing American lifestyles met a captivating
young nurse named Sheila Larson. "I
believe in God," Sheila told her interview-
er. "However, I'm not a religious fanatic. I
can't remember the last time I went to
church. My faith has carried me a long
way. It's 'Sheilaism.' Just my own little
voice."

Nadab and Abihu were just like Sheila.
God laid out in great detail the way He
was to be worshiped, but Aaron's sons
decided to do their own thing. Perhaps
they thought they could improve on God's
instructions. In any event, they chose to
come to God on their terms. They offered
"strange" or "profane" fire on the altar.
They rejected God's authority and God's
will; His response was to destroy them.

Many people today are trying to come
to God on their own terms. They believe in

God but they have their own way of reaching Him. Some seek to find God in nature; others are hoping to gain His approval through good works. God, however, has made it very clear that there is only one way to reach Him—through Jesus Christ. The Savior said, "I am the way, the truth, and the life. No one comes to the Father except through Me" (John 14:6).

Don't be fooled by those who tell you that there are "many ways to God." God has declared that there's only one— through His Son, Jesus. We either come God's way or not at all. There's no place for "doing your own thing."

The one way to God is the Son-way.

Reflections/Prayer Requests

_____

_____

_____

_____

_____

_____

_____

_____

_____

_____

DAY 15

Leviticus 16:7-10

He shall take the two goats and present them before the LORD at the door of the tabernacle of meeting. Then Aaron shall cast lots for the two goats: one lot for the LORD and the other lot for the scapegoat. And Aaron shall bring the goat on which the LORD's lot fell, and offer it as a sin offering. But the goat on which the lot fell to be the scapegoat shall be presented alive before the LORD, to make atonement upon it, and to let it go as the scapegoat into the wilderness.

My Sins Far Away

The star nearest to our solar system is the triple star Proxima Centauri, located about 25 trillion miles from earth. Even though it is our nearest neighbor, it's still so far away that it takes the light from Proxima Centauri more than four years to reach us traveling at the speed of 186,282 miles per second. That's an incredible distance, but it's nothing when compared to the distance which God separates us from our sins.

God instructed Moses on the protocol for making a sin offering. He must take two goats. One would be sacrificed as a sin offering. The other, called the scapegoat, was sent away into the wilderness, symbolically carrying the sins of the people with it. Physically the wilderness was not that far away, but spiritually those sins were carried so far that they would never be found again.

The psalmist declares, "As far as the east is from the west, so far has He removed our transgressions from us" (Ps 103:12). No distance on earth can be farther than the distance that east is from west. No greater gulf can exist than the gulf between ourselves and our sin when we are forgiven by our Holy God.

If you have placed your sins under the blood of Christ, rest assured that they will never be found again. They have been carried beyond the farthest stars and they will never return.

The only thing farther away than far-off stars are forgiven sins.

Reflections/Prayer Requests

_____

_____

_____

_____

_____

_____

_____

_____

_____

DAY 16

Leviticus 16:29-30

*This shall be a statute forever for you:
In the seventh month, on the tenth day
of the month, you shall afflict your souls,
and do no work at all, whether a native
of your own country or a stranger who
sojourns among you. For on that day the
priest shall make atonement for you, to
cleanse you, that you may be clean
from all your sins before the LORD.*

Cleanse Me

The resurgence of infectious diseases and their growing resistance to antibiotics are renewing the need for low-tech health practices like hand washing. Reports in the *Journal of the American Medical Association* and other medical journals cite studies that link outbreaks of bacterial and viral illness in hospitals, nursing homes and child-care centers to the absence of basic cleanliness.

In a similar fashion, what dirt does to our physical health, sin does to our spiritual health. That's why God instructed Moses to set aside a day each year called the Day of Atonement. On that day the high priest made a special sacrifice on behalf of the people that they might be cleansed from their sin. Their spiritual health depended on it.

In the New Testament, we don't need a special day for cleansing. Not only is the blood of Jesus sufficient to atone for our sins when we are born again, it is also continually available to clean up those spots of sin that splash onto our lives every day. The apostle John wrote, "the blood of Jesus Christ His Son cleanses us from all sin" (1 John 1:7).

If there is sin in your life, confess it to God today and claim the blood of Christ. Your spiritual health depends on it.

A cleansed Christian is a healthy Christian.

Reflections/Prayer Requests

_____

_____

_____

_____

_____

_____

_____

_____

_____

_____

_____

DAY 17

Leviticus 17:11

For the life of the flesh is in the blood, and I have given it to you upon the altar to make atonement for your souls; for it is the blood that makes atonement for the soul.

At-One-Ment

A Japanese soldier named Shoichi Yokoi lived in a cave on the island of Guam. He fled there in 1944 when the tides of war began to change. Fearing for his life, he stayed hidden for 28 years, coming out only at night. During this time, he lived on frogs, rats, snails, shrimp, nuts and mangoes. Even when he figured out the war was over, he was afraid to come out for fear he would be executed. Two hunters found him one day and escorted him to freedom. He had lived all this time under condemnation for wrongs that had been dealt with. Forgiveness had been granted, but he failed to apply the benefits of this armistice to his life.

As God began to build the nation that would become His chosen people, He charted the way they could approach Him without condemnation. It was through blood. The blood which represented the life of the one sacrificed would be the "atonement for your souls." Through a blood offering, the one making the sacrifice could be "at one" with God.

The Hebrew word translated as *atonement* means "to cover." The Old Testament animal sacrifices were intended to "cover" a man's sins. In the New Testament, the concept of atonement is expressed by the word *expiate*, which means "to put away." That's a significant step forward in the meaning of salvation. The blood that Jesus shed for us at Calvary does not merely cover up our sin; it puts away our sin as though it had never been committed.

If you find yourself living in a spiritual exile, isn't it time you received God's atonement, the sacrifice of His own Son for you? Jesus paid the penalty for your sin with His own blood. Let Him make you eternally at one with God.

Christ's atonement is the key to God's at-one-ment.

Reflections/Prayer Requests

DAY 18

Leviticus 19:1-2

And the LORD spoke to Moses, saying, "Speak to all the congregation of the children of Israel, and say to them: 'You shall be holy, for I the LORD your God am holy.'"

Keep Your Distance

Have you heard the story about the wealthy gentleman who was interviewing applicants for the position of chauffeur? After speaking with a number of candidates, he narrowed the field down to three finalists. He asked each man the same question: "How close do you think you could drive to a thirty-foot drop-off? The first said six feet. The second said three feet. The third, however, replied, "I don't know, but I'd stay as far away as I could." You can guess which one got the job. When it comes to some risks, it's best to keep your distance.

The same is true of sin. As God gave Israel His standards for living, He based them on one essential truth: He is a holy God. As His people, Israel also needed to reflect this holiness. The word used for "holy" carries the idea of being "separate." God and sin cannot coexist. Therefore, the Israelites were to live in such a way that they would avoid the contamination of sin. While God realized that they could not reach His level of purity, He still expected them to separate themselves and not participate in the sinful lifestyles of the nations around them.

In the New Testament, the call for holiness becomes even more personal. The word *saints*, when used for believers, literally means "holy ones." We are to separate ourselves from our old lives of sin and live new lives of righteousness.

If you know that you have a weakness in a particular area, keep your distance. If it's pornography, stay away from places where it's sold. If it's gossip, avoid those people who may feed you information that you'll be tempted to pass on. The farther you stay away from sin, the easier holiness will be.

A long distance is sometimes the shortest path to holiness.

Reflections/Prayer Requests

_____

_____

_____

_____

_____

_____

_____

_____

DAY 19

So Moses said to the LORD, "Why have You afflicted Your servant? And why have I not found favor in Your sight, that You have laid the burden of all these people on me?"

Heavy Burdens

When our burdens get heavy, it's tempting to dump our responsibilities. In Jacksonville, Florida, two women on their way to work found a naked infant, believed to be less than an hour old, on the side of an interstate. The women brought the infant boy to a nearby hospital, where he was reported to be in good condition. A 24-year-old woman in Dallas, Texas, abandoned her two little girls, ages 3 and 5, in a deserted warehouse frequented by a number of homeless men. When it became apparent that the mother was not returning, one of the homeless men took the girls to a county probation office, where arrangements were made to care for them more properly.

Moses faced the same temptation. Soon after leaving Egypt, the people began to complain. They accused Moses of trying to kill them (Ex. 14:11); they grumbled about the lack of water (15:22-24); they threatened to stone him (17:4); and they wept because they were tired of manna and wanted "the cucumbers, the melons, the leeks, the onions, and the garlic" of Egypt (Num. 11:5). After suffering through these and many other problems, Moses was ready to quit; in fact, he said to God, "If You treat me like this, please kill me here and now" (v. 15).

Fortunately, God had a better idea. He instructed Moses to find 70 men who would help him carry the burden of these cantankerous people (vv. 16-17). With their help, Moses continued on for another 40 years.

If you are trying to bear a burden by yourself—don't! That's something God's people are suppose to do together (Gal. 6:2). If you know of someone who is bearing a burden, go to him and offer to help. Heavy burdens were never meant to be shouldered alone. Help someone bear a burden today.

A burden shared is a lighter load.

Reflections/Prayer Requests

_____

_____

_____

_____

_____

_____

_____

DAY 20

Numbers 12:1-2

Then Miriam and Aaron spoke against Moses because of the Ethiopian woman whom he had married . . . . And they said, "Has the Lord *indeed spoken only through Moses? Has He not spoken through us also?" And the* Lord *heard it.*

The Error of Envy

Irish novelist and playwright Samuel Beckett received great recognition for his work, but not every one appreciated his success. Beckett's marriage, in fact, was soured by his wife's jealousy of his growing fame as a writer. One day in 1969 his wife answered the telephone, listened for a moment, spoke briefly and hung up. She then turned to Beckett and with a stricken look whispered, "What a catastrophe!" It turned out that she had just learned that her husband had been awarded the Nobel Prize for Literature!

Aaron and Miriam, Moses' brother and sister, were guilty of the same kind of jealousy. When Moses took a new wife, these two began to voice their objections. Perhaps they were afraid this woman would have too much influence; perhaps they were fearful she would steal Moses' affections away from them. Whatever the excuse, their hearts were filled with jealousy and they began to speak against their brother. In response, God called the three of them to a meeting at the tabernacle. At the end of this divine confrontation, Miriam was afflicted with leprosy (v. 10). The jealousy eating her up on the inside became a disease that consumed her on the outside. Only Moses' intercessory prayer spared her a horrible death.

Jealousy can still be found in the hearts of Christians today, and the consequences are just as terrible. Jealousy over who gets to sing the solo in the church Christmas cantata has torn choirs apart. Envy over a sister who is more popular or a brother with a better job has driven wedges between siblings. Sometimes even parents have been jealous of their own children.

If you are aware of jealousy in your heart, root it out at once. Confess it as sin. Seek to do good toward those you envy. The longer you let jealousy linger, the more damage it will do—to you, and everyone else.

As rust destroys metal, so jealousy destroys people.

Reflections/Prayer Requests

DAY 21

Numbers 14:4

So they said to one another, "Let us select a leader and return to Egypt."

The Rebellious Heart

After the news leaked out that George Bush banned broccoli aboard Air Force One, a group of broccoli growers sent 10 tons of the vegetable free to Washington, D.C. With rebellion dripping from his words, the president reiterated his distaste with gusto: "I do not like broccoli and I haven't liked it since I was a little kid and my mother made me eat it. And I'm president of the United States, and I'm not going to eat any more broccoli."

The nation of Israel, however, was rebelling against something far more serious than a vegetable—they were rebelling against God. When 10 of the 12 spies returned with a negative report concerning the land of Canaan, the people rose up in arms. Joshua and Caleb, the two spies who brought back a positive report, begged the people, "Do not rebel against the LORD" (Num. 14:9). Their plea, however, fell on deaf ears and God's wrath burned against the people. He told Moses, "I will strike them with the pestilence and disinherit them, and I will make of you a nation greater and mightier than they" (v.12). Through Moses' intercession, the people were spared, but every adult over the age of 20 was condemned to wander in the wilderness until all that generation died except for Joshua and Caleb.

The Bible says, "Rebellion is as the sin of witchcraft" (1 Sam 15:23). Since witchcraft was one of the crimes punishable by death in those days, it's obvious that the Lord does not regard rebellion lightly. God still sees rebellion as a serious sin.

Is there some rebellion in your heart against God? Are you rebelling against some difficult circumstance that He has allowed to come into your life? Perhaps it's sickness, financial problems or family difficulties. No matter what the problem is, the consequences of rebellion are far too dreadful to nurture such an attitude. Instead, submit your life to the Lord. Go on with what you know is His will for you, and trust Him to work out all of the other challenges in your life.

Fear makes a rebel; trust makes a saint.

Reflections/Prayer Requests

_____

_____

_____

_____

_____

DAY 22

Numbers 14:39-40

*Then Moses told these words
to all the children of Israel,
and the people mourned greatly.
And they rose early in the morning and went
up to the top of the mountain, saying, "Here
we are, and we will go up to the place which
the LORD has promised, for we have sinned!"*

Missed Opportunities

Some people are more attuned to opportunities than others. A youngster came home from selling Christmas cards one day. "How much did you make today?" his father asked. "Fifty dollars!" replied the young man. "Why, that's excellent," responded his father. "How many homes did you call on?" "Just one," the boy replied, "but their dog bit me." While we can't condone his approach, this fellow certainly knew an opportunity when he saw one.

Unfortunately, Israel didn't. God gave them a wonderful opportunity. If they would obey Him and enter the land He had promised, He would take care of all the obstacles. God promised to fight for them. Chariots of iron and fortified cities were no problem for Him. The Israelites' reaction, however, was to dig in their heels and refuse to obey. Later, after they realized their sin, it was too late. When they went out to do battle, Moses and the Ark of the Covenant, the symbol of God's presence in their midst, stayed in the camp. As a result, "the Amalekites and the Canaanites who dwelt in that mountain came down and attacked them, and drove them back as far as Hormah" (Num. 14:45). By delaying their obedience, they missed their opportunity and were doomed to wander in the wilderness for 40 years.

If the Lord is calling you to do something, don't delay. Doors of opportunity close as well as open. By failing to obey at once, you may lose the possibility to obey at all. Be sensitive to God's leading, and follow it without reservation.

Delayed obedience is only another form of disobedience.

Reflections/Prayer Requests

_____

_____

_____

_____

_____

_____

_____

_____

DAY 23

Numbers 27:18-20

*And the L*ORD *said to Moses: "Take Joshua the son of Nun with you, a man in whom is the Spirit, and lay your hand on him; set him before Eleazar the priest and before all the congregation, and inaugurate him in their sight. And you shall give some of your author-ity to him, that all the congregation of the children of Israel may be obedient."*

Passing on Treasures

A family had a valuable antique vase that had been handed down through several generations. It was kept on the mantel in the living room as a special object of enjoyment. One day the mother came home and was greeted by her daughter's question, "Mother, you know that vase which you told us has been passed down from generation to generation?" "Yes," her mother acknowledged. "Well," said the girl, "this generation just dropped it."

When passing treasures to the next generation, a real danger exists that something we value might get dropped. Moses was aware of that. When it came time to pass the mantel of leadership on, God directed him specifically in how he should do it.

This process began with a worthy recipient. Moses was instructed to take Joshua, "a man in whom is the Spirit"

(v. 18). Furthermore, it was to be a public process before all the congregation (v. 19) so that no one could be accused of behind-the-scenes wheeling and dealing. And finally, it was a gradual process. Moses was to give *some* of his authority to Joshua (v. 20). This gave the young man the opportunity to begin to practice the art of leadership while still under the guidance of an experienced mentor.

Begin now to pass on to your loved ones those things that are of value to you. As a Christian, the most valuable asset you possess is your faith. Make sure your family knows where you stand with Christ. Share with them openly what your faith means to you. Encourage them and mentor them so that they can follow in your footsteps. Don't let the greatest treasure you possess get dropped.

Don't "pass on" without first passing it on.

Reflections/Prayer Requests

_____

_____

_____

_____

_____

_____

DAY 24

Numbers 35:9-12

*Then the L*ORD *spoke to Moses, saying, "Speak to the children of Israel, and say to them: 'When you cross the Jordan into the land of Canaan, then you shall appoint cities to be cities of refuge for you, that the manslayer who kills any person accidentally may flee there. They shall be cities of refuge for you from the avenger, that the manslayer may not die until he stands before the congregation in judgment.'"*

A Place of Refuge

Mistakes happen to everyone—and sometimes they're tragic. When the space shuttle *Challenger* lifted into the sky on a chilly Tuesday morning, January 28, 1986, and then exploded 73 seconds into its flight, everyone realized a terrible mistake had been made. Because of the cold weather, the O-ring seals on the booster rockets malfunctioned. Burning rocket propellant ignited an explosion in which seven people lost their lives. While not all mistakes are this disastrous, they still often leave us wondering what to do.

In God's plan for the nation of Israel, He established six cities as places of refuge. These were located strategically throughout the land, so that those who committed a crime accidentally, even if it involved killing someone, could flee there for safety. While in the confines of that city, he was safe from anyone who sought vengeance because of his mistake.

Mistakes—things done by accident with no intent to cause harm—demand our compassion. They may make us sad; they may even make us angry because of the lack of good judgment shown. But in the midst of it all, we must realize that humans are fallible creatures.

If you are the victim of a mistake, even a serious one, God calls you to forgiveness and compassion. The apostle Paul wrote, "Therefore, as the elect of God, holy and beloved, put on tender mercies, kindness, humbleness of mind, meekness, longsuffering; bearing with one another, and forgiving one another, if anyone has a complaint against another; even as Christ forgave you, so you also must do" (Col. 3:12-13). In His compassion, Christ offers us a refuge from our sins; for our part, we must offer others a refuge from theirs.

Lack of forgiveness for those who make mistakes is a mistake itself.

Reflections/Prayer Requests

_____

_____

_____

_____

DAY 25

Deuteronomy 1:3, 8

Now it came to pass in the fortieth year, in the eleventh month, on the first day of the month, that Moses spoke to the children of Israel according to all that the LORD had given him as commandments to them.
"See, I have set the land before you; go in and possess the land which the LORD swore to your fathers—to Abraham, Isaac, and Jacob—to give to them and their descendants after them."

A Time for Action

Two men were talking and one said, "Boy, there's nothing like getting up early in the morning, doing a few calisthenics, taking a vigorous three-mile run and then hitting the showers." "Oh," said the other man, "when did you start doing this?" "I haven't," replied his friend, "but I'm going to start one of these days."

"One of these days" finally arrived for Israel. For 40 years the people had wandered in the wilderness as the older generation died off. Moses had passed the mantel of leadership down to his young understudy, Joshua, and was preparing to meet with God on Mount Nebo, his final resting place. His last words to the people were a reminder and an exhortation. The way had been long, the battles fierce; but the time of waiting was over. Now was the time for action—go in and possess the land.

It is all too easy to let procrastination dominate our lives. There is a time to wait and pray, to study the situation, to make careful preparations—but there's also a time to take action. Dragging your feet is just as much a sin as running ahead of the Lord.

If God has been speaking to you about something, stop putting it off. Pray about it. Seek advice from your pastor and godly friends. Pray some more. Then, do something. Don't delay; obey.

"One of these days" can easily become none of these days.

Reflections/Prayer Requests

_____

_____

_____

_____

_____

_____

_____

_____

_____

_____

DAY 26

Deuteronomy 2:19-22

"And when you come near the people of Ammon, do not harass them or meddle with them, for I will not give you any of the land of the people of Ammon as a possession, because I have given it to the descendants of Lot as a possession." (That was also regarded as a land of giants; giants formerly dwelt there. But the Ammonites call them Zamzummim, a people as great and numerous and tall as the Anakim. But the LORD destroyed them before them, and they dispossessed them and dwelt in their place, just as He had done for the descendants of Esau, who dwelt in Seir, when He destroyed the Horites from before them. They dispossessed them and dwelt in their place, even to this day.)

Giant Killer

The realm of legend is filled with the myths of people who met and overcame giants. Such characters as Jack and the Beanstalk, Sinbad the sailor and Jack the Giantkiller all knew what it meant to face and conquer an enemy many times larger than they.

God, however, knows how to deal with giants for real. The Israelites who left Egypt failed to grasp this truth. When 10 of the 12 spies sent into Canaan returned with tales of giant warriors, which they called the Anakim (Num. 13:33), the people refused to go into the land (14:1-4).

Four decades later, as Moses prepared the descendants of that generation to face the gigantic descendants of their enemies, he reminded them of God's history of dealing with giants. God destroyed the Emim, a people as great and numerous as the Anakim, on behalf of the descendants of Lot (Deut. 2:9-10). He also annihilated the Horites, another race of giants, and gave their land to the descendants of Esau (v. 12). Even the Ammonites were given the land of the giants, which they called the Zamzummim (vv. 19-20).

Are you facing some giants in your life: sickness, an uncertain future, a troubled marriage, financial woes? Do what Moses did. Trust God. Ask for His help in destroying your giants. He is quite able to deal with those things that are bigger than you.

All giants are dwarfed in God's sight.

Reflections/Prayer Requests

_____

_____

_____

_____

_____

_____

_____

DAY 27

Deuteronomy 4:2

*You shall not add to the word which I command you, nor take anything from it, that you may keep the commandments of the L*ORD *your God which I command you.*

Contamination Catastrophe

In August 1997, Hudson Foods issued the biggest recall of meat—an estimated 2.5 million pounds—in United States history. It was discovered that millions of pounds of meat processed in one of the company's factories were contaminated with the E. coli bacteria, which causes severe diarrhea, cramps and dehydration. In some cases, it can even cause death.

Contaminating God's Word can create an equally serious disaster when it comes to a person's spiritual life. Moses knew that when the Israelites settled down in the land God promised them, they would be surrounded by nations who worshiped other gods. Often these false religions involved human sacrifices and sexual immorality. Therefore, he warned the people against polluting the pure Word of God by adding any of those pagan beliefs or altering in any way the truths God had spoken to them.

Spiritual contamination is still a very real threat—and the consequences can be as catastrophic as E. coli. The Jonestown massacre, the Branch Davidian deaths and the Heaven's Gate suicides all demonstrate the deadliness of mixing error with God's truth. The apostle Paul warned the elders of the Ephesus church, "After my departure savage wolves will come in among you, not sparing the flock" (Acts 20:29), while the apostle John wrote, "Many deceivers have gone out into the world" (2 John 1:7). From the beginning of the church right up to today, some people have sought to taint the pure milk of the Word with their own poisonous additives.

When confronted by those who want to add or subtract from God's Word, when someone tells you that you need to buy their book in addition to God's Book, the safest response is to reject whatever they might have to offer. You can be sure that their contamination will make you ill and might even be fatal. God's Word is pure truth; let's keep it that way.

Tainted truth can be toxic.

Reflections/Prayer Requests

_____

_____

_____

_____

_____

DAY 28

Deuteronomy 10:12-13

And now, Israel, what does the LORD *your God require of you, but to fear the* LORD *your God, to walk in all His ways and to love Him, to serve the* LORD *your God with all your heart and with all your soul, and to keep the commandments of the* LORD *and His statutes which I command you today for your good?*

All to Jesus

The term "the whole nine yards" came from World War II fighter pilots in the South Pacific. The .50 caliber machine gun ammunition belts they used measured exactly 27 feet, before being loaded into the fuselage. If the pilots fired all their bullets at a target, it got "the whole nine yards." This has come to mean that you give something your complete effort.

As Moses prepared the people to enter the land of Canaan, he wanted to remind them of God's expectations—their complete effort. They were to fear the Lord, walk in His ways, love Him and serve Him with all their heart and soul. They were not to stop short but to give God "the whole nine yards."

God is never pleased with anything short of our total effort. Christ told the church at Laodicea, "I know your works, that you are neither cold nor hot. I could wish you were cold or hot. So then, because you are lukewarm, and neither cold nor hot, I will vomit you out of My mouth" (Rev 3:15-16). God's desire is for total commitment. He wants His people to give Him their all. Anything less is unacceptable.

The hymn writer says it this way: "All to Jesus I surrender; all to Him I freely give." Let that be your prayer today as you go "the whole nine yards" for Christ. In whatever you do, do it for Him with "all your heart and with all your soul."

With Jesus, all the way is the only way.

Reflections/Prayer Requests

_____

_____

_____

_____

_____

_____

_____

_____

_____

_____

_____

DAY 29

Deuteronomy 18:21-22

And if you say in your heart, "How shall we know the word which the LORD *has not spoken?"—when a prophet speaks in the name of the* LORD, *if the thing does not happen or come to pass, that is the thing which the* LORD *has not spoken; the prophet has spoken it presumptuously; you shall not be afraid of him."*

Sanctified Liars

A young woman was soaking up the sun's rays on the beach when a little boy came up to her and asked, "Do you believe in God?" She was surprised by the question but replied, "Why, yes, I do." "Do you go to church every Sunday?" he inquired. Again, her answer was "Yes!" Then he asked, "Do you read your Bible and pray every day?" Again she said, "Yes!" At last the boy sighed and said, with obvious relief, "Will you hold my quarter while I go in swimming?"

There is an expectation that those who claim to be religious will also be honest, but, sadly, that isn't always the case. God warned the Israelites that there would arise those who claimed to be prophets—spokesmen for God—yet the messages they delivered would be false. The people would know this because the things they prophesied would not take place. False prophecy was so serious that under the Old Testament law a person who prophesied falsely was to be put to death (Deut. 13:5, 18:20).

Under the dispensation of grace, we no longer stone false prophets, but we are still responsible for discerning them. The apostle John said, "Beloved, do not believe every spirit, but test the spirits, whether they are of God; because many false prophets have gone out into the world" (1 John 4:1). Those who are true spokesmen for God will appreciate such testing. The apostle Paul called the Bereans "fairminded" because they "searched the Scriptures daily to find out whether these things were so" (Acts 17:11).

Never make assumptions; let God's Word be your standard of truth. If someone tells you something that doesn't agree with the Bible, you can be sure it's a lie. God is true; His Word is true; those who disagree are not true. It's just that simple.

God's Light puts lies to flight.

Reflections/Prayer Requests

_____

_____

_____

_____

DAY 30

Deut 30:15-16

*See, I have set before you today life
and good, death and evil, in that I command
you today to love the* LORD *your God,
to walk in His ways, and to keep His commandments, His statutes, and His judgments,
that you may live and multiply; and the* LORD
*your God will bless you in the land
which you go to possess.*

Real Life

Reportedly, employees in a Detroit
business office found the following important notice on the bulletin board: "The
management regrets that it has come to
their attention that workers dying on the
job are failing to fall down. This practice
must stop, as it becomes impossible to
distinguish between death and the natural
movement of the staff."

While this memo was meant to be
humorous in a business setting, it's all too
serious in the spiritual setting. Moses
reminded the people that if they wanted a
real life, they needed to love the Lord,
walk in His ways and keep His commandments, statutes and judgments. Such a life
God will bless and make fruitful.

Many people walking our streets, shop-
ping in our malls and working beside us
are spiritually dead. You man never know
this simply by looking at them. They do all

the things that living people do, but in that spiritual part of their being, which was designed to fellowship with God, they have no life. They have a semblance of life, but they don't have God's life.

Jesus said, "The thief does not come except to steal, and to kill, and to destroy. I have come that they may have life, and that they may have it more abundantly" (John 10:10). Jesus offers us a life that is real. And not only real, but also abundant and full. Real life doesn't come in finding yourself; it comes in finding Him. Love Him, keep His commands and really live.

Living is biological; life is spiritual.

Reflections/Prayer Requests

DAY 31

Deuteronomy 34:1, 4

*Then Moses went up from the plains
of Moab to Mount Nebo, to the top of Pisgah,
which is across from Jericho. And the LORD
showed him all the land.
Then the LORD said to him, "This is the land
of which I swore to give Abraham, Isaac, and
Jacob, saying, 'I will give it to your descendants.' I have caused you to see it with your
eyes, but you shall not cross over there."*

Mercy Me!

According to French historians, a
mother visited Napoleon on behalf of her
condemned son. The emperor told her the
young man had committed the same
offense twice, and justice demanded the
death penalty. "But Sire," she pleaded, "I
don't ask for justice—only for mercy." "He
doesn't deserve it," Napoleon replied. "No,
he doesn't," she admitted, "but it would
not be *mercy* if he deserved it." "You're
right!" said the ruler. "I'll grant your
request and show him mercy!"

On more than one occasion Moses let
his anger lead him into sin. It was anger
that caused him to kill the Egyptian
taskmaster (Ex. 2:11-12). Later God
instructed him to speak to the rock and it
would produce water. In his anger at the
people, Moses struck the rock instead.
Consequently, God said, "Because you did

not believe Me, to hallow Me in the eyes of the children of Israel, therefore you shall not bring this congregation into the land which I have given them" (Num. 20:12). God's justice required a consequence, but His mercy tempered those results. Even though Moses could not enter the land, God gave him the opportunity to see it from the top of Mount Pisgah.

The old hymn is right: "There's a wideness in God's mercy like the wideness of the sea; There's a kindness in His justice which is more than liberty." God is good at being merciful, just as He is good at being just.

If you feel like there is no hope for you because of your sin, remember God's mercy. You may bear the consequences of those transgressions, but God will not cast you out. Throw yourself on His mercy.

Mercy is not an excuse to sin, but it is our only hope when we do sin.

Reflections/Prayer Requests

_____

_____

_____

_____

_____

_____